EGON PUBLISHERS LTD

ISBN: 978 0905858 33 3

First published in UK: 1985
Revised and Reprinted: 2001
This Edition revised and reprinted 2007

Egon Publishers Ltd
618 Leeds Road
Outwood
Wakefield WF1 2LT
Tel: 01924 871697
FAX: 01924 871697
www.egon.co.uk

Egon Publishers Ltd
is owned and operated by
SEN Marketing
www.senbooks.co.uk

Blight, Jean

Practical guide
to dyslexia :
specific
                  371.
                  914
1793167

Also available in the same series:

A Practical Guide to Specific Learning Difficulties
ISBN: 978 1904160 84 7

For more details please visit:
www.senbooks.co.uk

JEAN BLIGHT

Mrs. Jean Blight is an experienced Teacher who was trained at Avery Hill Training College in London. Since then, she has taught in Infant and Junior Schools and a College of Further Education. She taught in a special school for ten years. She was the Assistant Director of the Watford Dyslexia unit from its foundation in January 1982 until September 1985, when she became the Director. Since April 1990 she has been Head of Special Help at Beechwood Park School. She retired in 1998 but continues to teach and assess pupils.

Different forms of Dyslexia

Dyslexia is the name given to difficulties in learning to read, comprehend and write. It affects a minority of children who are exposed to the normal processes of education and who do not show delay in other school subjects.

Dyscalculia is the difficulty some people have when working with numbers, their values, their sequences, tables and working out problems.

Dsygraphia is the problem some people have in writing symbols in an acceptably recognised form.

In music, reading of musical notation is a problem for some people, as is learning to play the piano which is more complicated as students have to learn two staves instead of one, as for a string or wind instrument.

Introduction

1. This booklet is intended as a simple guide for parents, teachers, speech therapists, doctors, health visitors and dyslexics themselves, to give them insight into, and understanding of the problem of dyslexia.

2. The word 'dyslexia' has been used because it is less cumbersome than the term 'specific learning difficulties' and better understood by the majority of people in the country at the present time. Gradually, the term 'specific learning difficulties' is becoming more widely used, especially by professional people such as Educational Psychologists. It is also used in many other countries such as America, Canada, Australia and New Zealand. Specific learning difficulties is the term more generally used in schools. However dyslexia is still used frequently in the media and by the public.

3. The list of signs of dyslexia is given for the different age groups. If it is suspected that a child or student has dyslexia and they are found to have four or more signs, which are persistent, it could be worth seeking professional advice.

4. If dyslexia is diagnosed, it can be helped greatly by sympathetic teaching, preferably on a one-to-one basis. With a great deal of hard work and co-operation on the part of the student, success can be achieved. This specialist teaching should:

    (a) be multisensory - which means using to the full the senses of hearing, sight and touch and sound.

    (b) be carefully structured so that the student achieves success at every stage

    (c) be above all, systematic and sympathetic. There must be a great deal of reinforcement throughout the teaching programme.

    (d) recognise that each pupil has strengths and weaknesses. The teaching should take these into account and adapt accordingly.

5. It is very important that dyslexics are encouraged to practise and develop their skills at all times, otherwise they will lose their hard gained achievements and it will take further intensive effort to recover their previous position. They will have bad days, when they seem unable to remember things that they previously learnt. Fortunately, these times pass. To live with dyslexia is to accept that there is a problem, and to find ways of learning to cope and means of compensating.

6. Children with these difficulties are inclined to be very demanding, but are often very loving and sensitive too. They require a lot of time and patience. If they are encouraged to talk about problems as they arise, they will be able to come to terms with their disability, so becoming happier and more confident individuals. This support is required for a very long time and can't be hurried. However they do 'take off' and become confident people in their own right.
7. People with this condition should at all times remember that there are many other dyslexics in the world coping with their own special problems. They must realise that although reading, spelling, writing, maths or music can be more difficult for them than for other people, they still have much to offer. They have many special strengths which they should always be encouraged to develop to the full. Their intelligence and normality in every other sphere of life must be emphasised at all times, so that they can fulfil their potential. They can be stubborn at times, but they need this characteristic to succeed and survive. They usually know what is right for them, and this must be respected.
8. In conclusion, dyslexics have a lot going for them and they can succeed in life, even though it may take a little longer.

Signs of dyslexia in the five-seven age group

1. Early speech problems - difficulties in pronouncing words correctly and getting words into the right sequence. Sometimes the development of language skills has been slow, but children can be very articulate and may develop an excellent vocabulary.
2. Learning and remembering rhymes may be difficult. Recognition of similar words, such as ball and call, may be a problem.
3. Difficulty in hearing different sounds such as bpd, gj, uy, fvth.
4. Early learning problems -lack of attention when spoken to -lack of interest in listening to stories and failure to understand when explanations are given.
5. Lack of progress in reading, writing and spelling, contrary to expectations built up by normal development in other areas.
6. Although they appear bright in many ways, they may find it incomprehensible that words can only be read in one way. For example, they argue that whichever way one looks at a pair of spectacles, they are still spectacles. They do not understand that there is only one way to read the word 'spectacles'.

7. Poor motor control - for example, difficulty when using scissors and holding a pencil, and keeping within guide lines when colouring pictures.
8. Mirror writing and difficulty in forming letters and writing them down in some reasonable order. Constant confusion with bdp, gj, uy, mn, sz.
9. No sense of left and right.
10. Trouble with deciding which hand to use when eating, drawing, playing, throwing balls, etc.
11. Clumsiness when moving and lack of dexterity.
12. Difficulty in remembering instructions e.g. "Go upstairs and get me your blue sweater and bring it down with my book which is in my bedroom."
13. Difficulty in knowing the time of day and the sequence of events, e.g. forgetting that they had had their breakfast. Also, personal details such as the date of their birthday and their home address.
14. Counting may be hard work; they need to use sticks or fingers to help them.
15. Difficulty in playing sequencing and matching games.
16. Problems with doing up buttons, zips, tying shoe laces, and with the order in which they put their clothes on.
17. Tantrums and signs of frustration at home, and at school for no apparent reason.
18. Daydreaming and switching off in class and at home.
19. Reluctance to go to school after a happy start.
20. If any literacy problems have already occurred in the family then special attention should be given to the signs given above.

Things to do to help the five-seven age group

1. Talk to them, explain clearly and listen with great care to their answers, correcting them gently but not too frequently.
2. If speech is late in developing, or if there are problems to do with incorrect word order in a sentence, lack of understanding, or general immaturity of speech, seek the help of the local Speech Therapist.
3. If literacy skills are slow in developing, have eyesight and hearing checked.
4. Read to them and be persistent. It may take a long time before they will listen and follow the story. Start with simple repetitive stories that they can join in. Stories on cassettes are an enjoyable and useful aid. Above all, make stories fun.

5. Sing songs together. Say and read poems, rhymes and jingles.

6. Encourage them to paint and gradually develop this into writing and drawing. Encourage them to write from left to right and form their letters correctly, which means starting all the letters on the line by adding a 'tail'. This helps them to develop cursive writing much more easily at a later date.

7. Help them to recognise their name in writing. Encourage the use of lower case script i.e. small letters in the proper places. Teach them to say their address clearly and how to write it down.

8. Teach the sounds of the letters (not the names) and relate them to the symbols. Lower case letters should be taught first, followed by upper case letters, for example the sound 'a' (as in cat) should be related to a and A.

9. Make reading fun by reading with them using paired reading where the adult reads quietly at the same time as the child. This enables the children to hear the story and make sense of what they are reading. Read alternate pages. Read to them missing out words, which they have to put in quickly. Then they can do it, so they don't lose face if they don't know the word. Read regularly in short bursts and stop when concentration wanes. However, be delighted when they read more than expected. Keep the reading material at their level and gradually increase their reading level, so they feel successful all the time.

10. Start counting things and putting them in pairs and groups. Make a collection of similar things and those that are different. Introduce number through counting - using everyday objects sllch as spoons, mugs etc. Show them how to write numbers correctly and encourage them to recognise them in everyday life e.g. house numbers, prices, 30 m.p.h.

11. Emphasise sequencing and listening to numbers e.g. twenty-three, making sure that the 2 is written down first followed by the 3. The teen numbers often prove difficult, so teaching them by saying 17 is 7 in the units place and 'teen' in the ten's place can help. Unfortunately the reverse is true for the rest of the numbers, but a lot of reinforcement can overcome this difficulty.

12. Help by talking about the days of the week, and what happen on them e.g. Monday - swimming, Tuesday - visit Granny. Follow by introducing the months of the year - birthdays, festivals, seasons - stressing the sequencing all the time.

13. Discuss groups of animals, plants and everyday objects into the appropriate categories, e.g. table, chair, couch and desk are furniture.

14. Begin working on the recognition of right and left. Use songs and rhymes to reinforce the idea e.g. "1, 2, 3,4,5, Once I caught a fish alive," etc. Put shoes, boots in the right position saying "left" and "right" as they put them on. Set the table, emphasising the knife on the right and fork on the left.

15. Show clearly the sequence of putting on clothes and teach them how to cope with buttons, zips, press studs, ties, shoe laces. Choose clothes with the minimum of problems at first, but persist until all the necessary skills are learnt.

16. Play ball games, sequencing, matching and board games as a family and show your delight when they are successful and especially when they show signs of improvement.

17. Jigsaws are useful aids which help understanding of pictures and how ideas develop.

Signs of dyslexia in the seven-thirteen age group

1. Unable to read, or reading age well below chronological age.

2. Still having difficulty with sounds of letters.

3. Very inadequate spelling in written work, with a preference for using short familiar words. More complicated words are either spelt phonetically or by guesswork.

5. When reading aloud and writing, confusion among groups of letters such as bdp, gj, uy, wm, un, ij, ft, vf, th, still exists. Combinations of letters such as 'str' can still cause problems.

6. No idea of punctuation when reading or writing a story.

7. Essays and stories may often be brief and to the point, with very little description or development of the characters or story line.

8. If they can read but have little pleasure in this activity, and seem to hate books and reading aloud, this can cause great problems, e.g. missing change of tense and plurals and misreading small words such as saw and was.

9. Some children, even those who have a good reading age, have great problems in hearing the story or the information in their minds. This means that although they read the words accurately, they do not absorb the story line, or the information given, and so reading seems to be a waste of time. A slow reading rate also has the same effect.

10. Children at this age can often tell a story easily verbally, but they have a great struggle when it comes to writing it down on paper.
11. Copying from the blackboard is a problem. Lines are missed, letters and numbers are transposed. Some children also find the same difficulty when copying from a textbook.
12. They may still reverse numbers, e.g. writing 24 for 42 when doing complex arithmetic.
13. Great problems in remembering multiplication tables, particularly their sequence. Also, the order of the days of the week, months of the year and the alphabet.
14. Musical notation can prove problematical, and a lack of feeling for timing can occur. A string, brass or wind instrument is preferable to the piano.
15. Clumsiness and lack of co-ordination are still present.
16. Some dyslexic children appear to have difficulty in understanding what is said to them and there is a time-lag before they answer. They seem to have to translate the sentence into a language of their own to obtain the answer, then translate it into ordinary English.
17. At this stage, frustration, withdrawal and behavioural problems seem to be increasing.
18. Extreme reluctance to go to school may cause problems for all the family.

Things to do to help the seven-thirteen age group

1. If, at the age of seven plus, they are still having problems with reading, written work, spelling or mathematics, and yet seem bright in other ways, developing and growing normally, they need help.
2. Have their hearing and eyesight checked and, if all is well, go to the school and discuss the problems with the Head Teacher.
3. Help from the School Psychological Service could be offered. At this stage accept the help. It should be on a one-to-one basis, carefully structured and multisensory in approach. Keep a close eye on the child's progress. If you are not satisfied, look for a second opinion or look for alternative help.
4. Encourage them to develop interests of their own - swimming, art, making a collection, so that they feel they are succeeding. This will boost their self-confidence.

5. Children of this age group need a great deal of attention, reading to, talking to, listening to and working with. If this attention is given, it will help them to come to terms with their disability and accept it. They will then be encouraged to tackle the necessary hard work which will enable them to overcome their special problem.

6. Help them to get organised by making a timetable, putting down things they need e.g. Monday - violin, Tuesday - P.E. clothes etc. Be flnn that they do the remembering and make the preparations for the day.

7. Often their concentration span is limited, so it is important to gauge how long they can work easily. End the task before they lose concentration so preventing further frustration.

8. Remember that they tire easily and may need time doing very little in order to recover.

9. Some dyslexics have to concentrate very hard while watching television. This may be because, if they do not, they lose the thread of the story completely and it means nothing to them.

10. Encourage reading by letting them read easy books and comics but help them to develop this skill by introducing books with the minimum amount of print, gradually increasing this as they succeed. Let them read the books they want to read (Enid Blyton, for instance) not the books you would wish them to read.

11. Read aloud to them every day books that they should be reading but are failing to read. Encourage them to watch the text and get them to put in words which you miss out, while continuing to read. This helps eye movement. Then suggest firmly that they read a short passage at regular intervals. It can be helpful to use a piece of card to isolate the line being read, or point to the words with a pencil or finger. At suitable intervals, re-cap the events of the story in order to help them to remember the sequence of the story line, the characters involved, and to make sense of the text and to absorb and retain what they have heard.

12. Make sure that they know the days ofthe week, months ofthe year and help them with the alphabet. Show them how to use simple dictionaries and reference books.

13. Check that they can tell the time, using both the analogue and the digital clocks. If not, help in this area beginning with 0' clock and halfpast. Develop into the use of the 24 hour clock and its use in bus and train timetables.

14. Continue teaching multiplication tables. If this proves to be very difficult, teach the accurate use of a table card. It could help to explain the situation to the school. Persist in trying to get them to learn the tables. They are a valuable tool.

15. The use of squared paper is helpful when dealing with decimals. If the decimal point is in a square of its own then accurate addition, subtraction will follow, likewise when dealing with money.

16. Continue to play ball games and board and card games with them.

17. Check left and right confusion. Help by developing some compensating aid e.g. writing with right hand, wearing watch on the left.

18. The choice of secondary school is very important. If the children are still not coping and no help seems available, then this should be discussed with the new Head Teacher, Year Tutor or Counsellor to see what can be done.

19. Do not be reluctant to confess to the school that there is a family history of literacy problems.

20. At all times remember that parents know their children better than teachers. Try to be firm, polite but persistent in your efforts to get help. Do not forget, teachers are human too and can have difficulties in understanding a new situation, about which they may know very little.

Signs of dyslexia in the thirteen-eighteen age group

1. Frequent spelling mistakes still occur.

2. Copying from the blackboard can cause considerable difficulties. Typical problems include inaccurate copying, losing their place, and getting sentences muddled.

3. The planning of essays can prove a great burden because of the problem of the sequencing of ideas, and development of arguments. Choice of words may be restricted because of inhibitions over spelling.

4. Note-taking can be a problem - not understanding the main points and because of poor spelling. Note-taking from speech is especially difficult. They may be unable to make sense of their notes later, when needed for an essay, or for revision.

5. Understanding questions in comprehension. Exam questions can prove difficult because of the processes involved and ways of interpreting the information.

6. Reading rate may remain slow, therefore reading of any text at secondary level could cause problems.
7. French can prove problematical and discussion with the school would be advisable. Other foreign languages present fewer difficulties.
8. They still tire easily and need to relax or have a change of occupation to recuperate.
9. The level of their work can vary from excellent on one day to abysmal on another, according to how they feel.
10. Handwriting may still need attention and help.

Things to do to help the thirteen-eighteen age group

1. If they still need help - discuss the problem with them. If they agree, go ahead and find appropriate help. If unwilling, wait.
2. Encourage them to learn accurate typing skills, and to use computers and word processors. This will mean that they can produce a beautiful piece of work that looks really good.
3. Small hand held tape recorders can be useful to record lessons (with the teacher's permission) and for use when revising. Some people learn better through listening than through the written word.
4. Electronic notepads or laptop computers can be useful for recording homework details and other messages about school life, e.g. details of after school activities or games or music lessons.
5. 'Post it' notes can act as good reminders of things that need attention.
6. Teach mind mapping where links between concepts, rather than the sequencing of events is a priority. This helps with both essays and revision.
7. Good study skills and exam techniques are essential for these pupils.
8. Discuss with the school the choice and number of subjects to be taken in exams. Important factors in this choice are their interest, success already achieved in the subjects and their hopes for the future. To take fewer subjects and succeed, could be preferable to taking too many, which might lead to added pressure and possible failure.
9. Still encourage success in activities out of school e.g. football, chess, games, stamps etc. It is helpful if these activities include mixing with other people, as some dyslexics can find this a problem.
10. In the Summer term, before they begin their two year GCSE, contact the school and ask for details of the examining boards they will be using. The use of an amanuensis (handwriter) and or a computer is allowed in special circumstances. Additional help can also be given in

National Tests. Telephone or write to discover the allowances they make for dyslexic students and how these can be obtained. Discuss the pros and cons of having extra time with your children and abide by their wishes. This may need a full scale report from an Educational Psychologist and this must be done within a given time limit.

11. At a later date, when applying for jobs and colleges and universities, discover as much as is possible about the job or courses so that the young person will have the maximum chance of fulfilling his potential.

12. When considering future careers look into all the possible ways of obtaining the chosen goal. Often it is helpful to choose a certificate or diploma course, rather than a degree. It may take longer to achieve the goal, but the steps would be easier. If the chosen course includes practical work and a written project, which can be done at the candidate's own pace and counts towards the exam, it could be very helpful.

13. People with dyslexia often seem to mature later than their friends, so they still need a great deal of listening to, and encouraging, and even a gentle bullying to keep them going.

14. This can be a hard time for concerned parents because so often all that can be done is to stand back and watch. Young people can be very stubborn about accepting help and if they do not want it, then it will not benefit them at all. This probably causes further distress all round if they are made to receive it. Rejoice greatly with their successes and commiserate with their failure.

Signs of dyslexia in adults

1. Hopefully by the time they become adults they will have had help and be coping well and not afraid to be open about it. If they do have a bad day then they should be able to accept it and discuss it with the people concerned e.g. employers or lecturers.

2. Those who have not had the right help may be covering up their difficulties and compensating in all sorts of ways - such as taking home forms to fill in, not writing letters, etc.

3. They may still have great difficulties in taking instructions, in following conversations where the subject is changed, or in losing concentration suddenly; and completely forgetting what has happened or been said.

4. They may have problems in putting across their ideas to other people.

5. They dread parties in case word games are played.

6. They often pay bills with cash so as not to use a cheque book.

7. They often say a similar word instead of the correct one; they have never heard it correctly in the first place and cannot get their tongue round it properly e.g. cerstificate instead of certificate, cupboard for covered.

Things to do to help adults

1. Dyslexia is a condition for life, so they will always need encouragement and support to keep their hard gained skills in reading, writing, spelling and maths.
2. If they have not had the correct help in the past and have come to the stage in their careers where they need additional literacy skills, they should be encouraged to find help. This should be given by someone trained to teach dyslexics and should be on a one-to-one basis. Throughout this period they must be given every opportunity to succeed. Great patience and understanding may be needed. They must be treated by the tutor as an equal, intelligent adult - never as anything less. With hard work and determination adult dyslexics can make good progress.
3. If the correct documentation is presented at Universities/Colleges there are grants available to help with the purchase of computers. Some University Colleges also have Support Tutors who can give assistance.
4. Families and husbands and wives of dyslexics can be of the utmost help to them, but they must understand the limitations of the condition, and accept them, and help them in a very positive way to overcome their difficulties and find ways of compensating.
5. Dyslexia can and does run in families, so it is essential to watch for its occurrence in the next generation and to take the necessary steps to get the correct help in the early stages.
6. A form of dyslexia can occur after illness, such as strokes. This is called "acquired dyslexia" and needs a very specialised multi-disciplinary approach to overcome it.
7. At all times dyslexics must try and be positive about their achievements. On bad days they must remember how much better they are now than they were in the past, and how many goals they have achieved.
8. It is a great step forward if they can accept that spelling or writing or maths is not their particular strong point, and can make a joke about it without feeling to deflated. Remember that most people have some special difficulty particular to them, and everybody has bad days.

Book List

A wide selection of books on dyslexia can be obtained from:

SEN Marketing
618 Leeds Road
Outwood
Wakefield   WF1 2LT
Tel/FAX: 01924 871697
www.senbooks.co.uk

Desktop Publications
5 Laneham Street
Scunthorpe
North Lincs   DN15 6LJ
Tel: 0845 130 7413 FAX: 0845 130 7423
www.desktoppublications.co.uk

Organisations which will help dyslexics

British Dyslexia Association
98 London Road
Reading
Berks.   RG1 5AU
Helpline: 0118 966 8271
Tel: 0118 966 2677
FAX: 0118 935 1927
www.bdadyslexia.org.uk

Dyslexia Action
Park House
Wick Road
Egham
Surrey   TW20 0HH
Tel: 01784 222300
FAX: 01784 222333
www.dyslexiaaction.org.uk

Helen Arkell Dyslexia Centre
Frensham
Farnham
Surrey   GU10 3BW
Tel: 01252 792400
FAX: 01252 795669
www.arkellcentre.org.uk

Broxbourne Dyslexia Unit
The Priests House
90 High Road
Broxbourne
Tel: 01992 442002
More details on:
www.hertsdirect.org

The author wishes to thank her family, colleagues and friends for the support and interest. Special thanks to the friends who typed and sorted out her early efforts, especially to Mrs Mollie Seems and Anit Dalton for their help and assistance.